智慧的長河

釋迦牟尼

智慧的長河

釋迦牟尼

文／郝廣才　圖／保羅艾坦

Illustrations copyright © Paolo D'Altan, 1999

總編輯／郝廣才

責任編輯／劉思源・趙美惠

美術編輯／李燕玉

出版／格林文化事業股份有限公司

地址／台北市新生南路二段2號3樓

電話／(02)2351-7251　傳眞／(02)2351-7244

網址／www.grimmpress.com.tw

發行／易媒普有限公司

地址／高雄市金鼎路112號

電話／(07)310-1842　傳眞／(07)310-1843

ISBN／957-745-240-X

2000年12月初版1刷

2007年9月5刷

Great Names

智慧的長河

釋迦牟尼

文／郝廣才　圖／保羅艾坦

西元兩千五百年前， 在印度的北部，
誕生了一位偉大的聖哲。 人們稱他為
「佛陀」，意思是「 大徹大悟的人」。

佛陀的父親是迦毗羅衛城的國王，
稱為「 淨飯王」。迦毗羅衛城建築在
高高的山崖上， 遠看好像飄浮在空中
的城堡。 佛陀的母親是淨飯王的
王后， 名叫摩耶。

傳說摩耶王后有一晚， 夢見一隻白象
從月光通明的天空， 飛進她的床帳。
不久， 摩耶王后便懷孕了。

◆ 佛陀被尊稱為「釋迦牟尼」，牟尼是聖者、寂靜、苦修者的意思。

十戸個戈月世後戈， 在所一一次ち旅於行戸途交中戈， 摩迟耶世王孟后戈在所
一一棵丂大冬樹孟下Ⓧ， 產孝下Ⓧ一一個戈男孚孩所， 取名名迟為孟悉I達を多戈。
他を就戈是戸後戈來所的戈佛を陀さ。

　　據說他出生後沒多久，　有一位苦行僧求見
淨飯王。　當僧人看見悉達多時，　忍不住讚嘆道：
「國王陛下，　您的兒子將來會成為一個偉大的
聖哲，　他會捨棄王位出家修行，　唯有他才能讓
世上愚癡的人，　消除苦惱。　可惜我太老了，　不能
聽他說法，　真是可惜呀！」淨飯王聽了，　不禁
面露憂心之色。

　　悉達多漸漸長大，　不但會唸書，　又有很好的
武功。　淨飯王非常疼愛他，　他不希望兒子離開他，
所以刻意為他蓋了三座宮殿，　裡面全年開著鮮花，
服侍王子的人全部又年輕又漂亮。　淨飯王希望
兒子永遠生活在幸福快樂裡，　就不會想去出家。

　　悉達多從未見過外面的世界。　他從一個行宮
到另一個行宮時，　都坐在窗簾遮蓋的車轎裡。
他始終以為世上的一切，　都像他看見的那樣美好。

◆傳說佛陀七歲那年，淨飯王為他請了老師，教他印度最艱深的學問，例如養生之道、
　祭祀祝詞、兵法研究，以及有關工藝、醫學、宗教學等。並從十二歲開始學習武術，
　臂力驚人，在射箭方面真可說是百步穿楊。

　　悉達多十九歲那年，淨飯王在宮中舉行盛大的宴會，把全城的少女都請來。宴會中，悉達多愛上了美麗的雅蘇達拉。

　　淨飯王向雅蘇達拉的父親提親，但雅蘇達拉的父親要求悉達多必須通過他的考驗，他才願意把女兒嫁給悉達多。

　　第一項考驗是文藝。悉達多熟練的把六十四種經典背誦出來，輕鬆擊敗所有的參賽者。

　　第二項考驗是數學。悉達多正確的回答每一道問題。

　　第三項考驗是角力。悉達多將對手一一摔倒在地，無人能敵。

　　最後一項考驗是射箭。悉達多拉斷了所有的弓，最後，淨飯王從神廟中搬出一把沈重的大弓，悉達多拉動大弓，射出最後一枝箭。

悉達多通過考驗，
和雅蘇達拉舉行盛大婚禮，
婚宴持續十晝夜。

婚後，悉達多在
妻子的陪伴下，過著
更幸福快樂的生活。

但是有一天，悉達多
偶然走進花園，看見
園丁正在整理花圃，
換新的花苗。悉達多
好奇的問園丁在幹什麼？
園丁告訴他：「國王喜歡
在花朵凋謝前，就換上
新的花。」

「凋謝？」悉達多問，
「什麼是凋謝？」

園丁無法為他解釋

死亡的意義，只能傻傻一笑。

這一笑，像一顆小石子投進平靜的水面，只激起了
一陣小漣漪。不久，悉達多便忘了。

又有一天，悉達多聽見一個歌女在唱歌，聲音
很美，但他感覺有些怪，因為歌中有股憂愁，
悉達多從來不知道什麼是憂愁。

他問歌女唱的是什麼歌，歌女說：「這是描寫
我家鄉的歌。我的家鄉在很遠的地方，唱這首歌
讓我想起我的家鄉。」

悉達多心想：「世界上還有什麼地方，會比這裡
更讓人想念？為什麼我從沒想過到牆外去看看呢？」

於是悉達多對淨飯王說：「父王， 我想到宮外，看看外面的世界。」

　　寵愛悉達多的淨飯王， 只要兒子有要求， 沒有不答應的。 不過他預先做了準備。 他下令清掃街道， 把老人、 病人、 乞丐等聚集在一起， 遠離悉達多遊行的路線。

　　二十九歲生日這一天， 悉達多乘著三十六人抬的轎子， 帶著他心愛的白馬， 和他最親近的隨從車匿， 走出城門。

　　不管悉達多到哪裡， 他看到的都是漆著鮮明顏色的房子， 每個人都穿著漂亮的衣服， 又健康，又快樂。 人們向他拋撒玫瑰花瓣， 呼喊著他的名字。

　　悉達多非常興奮， 他不知道這一切其實都是淨飯王安排的表演。

◆佛陀之所以偉大在於他不是一個普通的革命者，因為一般的革命者大多是被欺壓的老百姓，為了
　過得更好，才起來推翻不合理的勢力。可是佛陀卻不一樣，他是為了解脫眾生煩惱，
　願意捨棄榮華富貴。這種不自私的情操實在令人敬佩。

正當悉達多要被護送回宮時，他忽然看見在一條小巷子裡，閃過兩個怪物。他們的身體很像人類，卻彎腰站立，好像腰折斷了似的，而且頭髮稀疏，皮膚上滿是皺痕，肋骨突出，張開口只有兩三顆黃牙……。

　　悉達多問車匿：「那是什麼東西？」

　　車匿回答：「是人啊！和我們一樣是人。」

「是人？人為什麼會長成那樣？」悉達多好驚訝。

車匿回答：「他們老了，殿下。」

「什麼是老？」

「年紀大了就會變老，所有的美麗、體力、記憶都會被老摧毀。每一個人都會老，沒有人逃得掉。」

　　原來人會老？花會凋謝？悉達多第一次想到這些，心裡非常難過，他默默無言的回到宮中。

◆佛陀發現人類最大的煩惱來自生老病死。他認為世間一切眾生都在六道輪迴裡浮沈，
　所謂六道指的是地獄、餓鬼、畜生、阿修羅（善於爭鬥的仙人）、人間及天神。
　生死就好像因果，每個人生前做了什麼事，死後就會輪迴到六道中受不同的苦，
　唯有超脫輪迴，才能享受真正的快樂。

　　年輕的王子心中有太多的疑問，　於是過了幾天，他騎著白馬再度和車匿出宮。　不久他們看見一個婦人在路旁不停咳嗽，　接著吐出一口髒東西，還發出刺鼻的惡臭。　悉達多非常吃驚，
問車匿：　「她怎麼了？」

「她很痛苦，　因為她病了！」

「病？」又是一個新字。

　　這時有人抬著腐爛的屍體走過，　白馬受到驚嚇，跳了起來。　悉達多又問：「那是什麼？」

　　車匿說：「殿下，　還是別知道的好。」

「快告訴我！」悉達多憤怒的說，「我命令你！」

車匿沒辦法，只好把悉達多帶到河邊。那裡有許多包著布的屍體，放在鋪著木柴和樹葉的平台上。有人將火點燃，熊熊烈火燒著屍體。

「這是死亡！殿下。」車匿說，「死亡就是和家人分離，結束生命，從這個世界消失。」

「每一個人都會死嗎？」悉達多問，「即使是國王也會死嗎？」

「是的，每個人都會死。國王、王子、公主和農夫、乞丐一樣都會死。」

　　悉達多懷著沈重的心情回到宮中，　卻發現有音樂在迎接他。　原來他的兒子出生了，　大家都在高興的慶祝。　但是悉達多的心頭卻好像壓著一顆大石頭，讓他笑也笑不出來。

　　因為人生的帷幕已經向他揭開，　他看到了人生恐怖的一面。　死亡和苦難映入他的眼中，　像惡夢般環繞著他。　他看到嬌豔的宮女，　便不由自主的想到，　她們轉眼間就會變成雞皮鶴髮的老太婆；新生的嬰兒也終將要面對生病、　衰老和死亡的階段。

　　半夜，悉達多自夢中驚醒，
他知道除非找到解決人生之謎
的方法，否則他無法快樂。

　　他決定捨下親愛的人，孩子、
妻子、父親……，這是
他第一次必須下這麼困難的
決定。但是如果他不離開，
這一輩子他都會是囚犯。

　　悉達多叫醒忠心的車匿，
把白馬的四蹄包上稻草
和棉布，兩人悄悄的出走。

悉達多和車匿離開迦毗羅衛城，不停的向前飛奔，最後在一處樹林中停下。悉達多跨下馬背，以誠懇的語氣對車匿說：「感謝你一直忠心耿耿的跟隨我，如今我們必須告別，請你回去吧。我要去找尋解脫生、老、病、死的方法。」

　　車匿流著眼淚，說：「可是您一旦離開皇宮，年老的國王，嬌弱的太子妃將會多麼的傷心，同時又有誰能教導您的孩子呢？您怎麼忍心拋棄自己的親人？」

悉達多說：「其實我最想掙脫的也正是這種痛苦呀！快樂恩愛似乎只是短暫的一場夢，人生免不了要有聚散離合。我想要解救所有人的痛苦，所以出家學道，假如我能成功，一定會回去的。」悉達多說完拔出寶劍，削斷他的長髮。

悉達多走入樹林，看見五個全身赤裸的男子。原來那五個男子是苦行僧，他們忍受飢餓寒冷，若不能悟出真理，便永遠不走出樹林。悉達多決定加入五個苦行僧，和他們一起修行。

六年多的時間裡，他們沒有講一句話，每天喝雨水，吃一點點野果，忍受風吹、雨打、日曬、蟲咬……悉達多變得骨瘦如柴，但是意志依然堅強。

　　有一天清晨，悉達多忽然聽見七絃琴和笛子的聲音。他睜開眼睛，看見一艘竹筏順流而下，上面坐著一老一少。老人吹著笛子，少年彈著七絃琴。突然，老人停止吹奏，對少年說：「絃不要上得太緊，否則它會繃斷的。」

　　這句話像鐘聲在悉達多的腦中迴盪，他忽然吃力的站起來，一步一步走向河邊。他在河中把自己的身體洗乾淨。這時一位好心的少女走來，端給他一碗粥。悉達多吃了幾口，他舉起碗對那五個苦行僧說：「來和我一起吃吧！上得太緊的絃是會繃斷的。」

　　五個苦行僧有的憤怒，有的吼叫，他們認為悉達多屈服於身體的慾望，紛紛轉身離他而去。

　　悉達多微微一笑，他知道過去的他和苦行僧都錯了。悉達多在一棵大樹下靜坐，他要往新的方向去思考，去悟出人生的真理。不知過了幾天幾夜，悉達多的眼前不斷出現惡魔、怪獸、美女等各種幻象。

悉達多努力靜心，幻象一一一消失。他睜開雙眼，看著天上的星星，一顆一顆，慢慢慢慢的，消失在晨光之中。

他的自我也隨著星星消失了。天是空的，他也是空的。悉達多悟出「空」的道理，自此他已成佛，成了大徹大悟的人。

佛陀成道後，他思考是否要將他悟出的道理傳給一般人？道理這樣難懂，一般人能夠了解嗎？……他決定要讓自己成為一艘船，載著眾生渡過生死苦難的長河。首先他便去找那五個苦行僧，向他們說法。這五個人成為佛陀最早的追隨者。佛陀也開始了他四十五年傳法的人生。

◆ 佛陀第一次說法，講的是四聖諦法門。內容大意是說，我們每個人一生都會面對許多苦，但只要我們了解自己，以正確的見解、純真的語言、真理的信仰等八種正道去修習，就能獲得解脫。

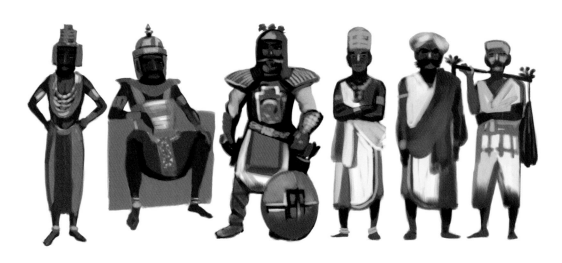

　　兩千五百年前的印度，　社會分成四個階段。　最高的是貴族和武士，　其次是僧侶，　再來是農人和商人，最低等的是奴隸，　也叫「賤民」，階級世世代代相傳，　永無翻身的日子。

　　印度教也和種姓階級有關。　宗教的經典，　只准前三個階級的人閱讀，　賤民是不允許知道的。　如果有人教賤民學習宗教經典，　不論那個人是什麼階級，都會受到嚴厲的懲罰。

　　佛陀決心打開一道新的門。　他認為眾生都是平等的，　並無階級之分。　他教導他的門徒不只要求自己解脫苦難，　也要幫助眾生解脫苦難。

　　他帶領門徒在恆河一帶，　向各種人說法傳道，不分貴賤，　不分貧富；　也接受來自不同階級的人的佈施。

佛陀常常用巧妙的方法，來講解他的道理。有一次，有個寡婦跑到佛陀那裡，非常哀傷的表示她唯一的兒子死了，她也不想活了。

　　佛陀笑著對她說：「你到村裡去，找一戶家裡從來沒有死過人的，向他們要一些芥菜籽，我就能解決你的苦難。」

　　婦人找遍村裡所有人家，每家人都願意給她芥菜籽，但沒有一家是家裡沒有死過人的。

　　婦人回來見佛陀，佛陀說：「芥菜籽呢？」

　　婦人跪在佛陀腳下，說：「你點化了我，我不會再要把孩子的生命找回來了。即使他復活，最後還是會死。教導我，讓我知道面對生死的道理吧！」

　　又有一次，有個人要殺一頭牛來拜神。佛陀對拜神的人說：「如果你感覺神給了你恩惠，那麼你應該犧牲自己回報神才對，這跟牛有什麼關係？為什麼要殘害牠？」

　　那人引用印度教經典的話，說：「經上說，動物如果在祭拜中被犧牲，動物的靈魂便會上天堂。所以我並沒有殘害牠，因為牠會上天堂啊！」

　　佛陀說：「既然可以因此而上天堂，那你為什麼不殺了你父親，或是你母親，還是你自己？你為什麼要放棄這個好機會？何況這頭牛也許不想上天堂呢！」

　　這人聽了，恍然大悟，他放下屠刀，對佛陀說：「你震驚了我，使我清醒，讓我知道自己過去的愚蠢。」

◆ 佛陀的教化講究自由平等的慈悲，也就是不論有沒有智慧、不分職業高低，只要聽從
　佛陀的教導，都能做佛陀的弟子，修成佛道。例如故事中的婦人和殺牛的人，都因為
　轉變思考方向而找到快樂的人生。

佛陀收了許多門徒，他把門徒當作種子，要他們把自己的宗教觀發揚光大。

　　佛陀在死前說的最後一句話是「沙馬沙提」，意思是：記住你是一個佛。他認為人人都可以成佛。今天他轉動了世界的輪子，當他停下時，輪子並不會停止，因為其他人可以接著轉下去。

　　佛陀雖然受到萬人的敬仰和追隨，但印度的貴族、僧侶和商人卻不喜歡他。他們竭盡全力破壞佛陀眾生平等的宗教觀，希望印度回到古舊的階級制度。

　　但是，佛陀的門徒越過喜馬拉雅山，將佛教傳進了中國，又傳到了日本、西藏、東南亞。今天，佛教是最多人信仰的宗教。佛陀的道理，也被許許多多「成佛」的人，一代代流傳下來。

作者介紹
郝廣才

　　郝廣才是台灣兒童書進入繪本時代的關鍵人物，他不但自己有非常豐富的創作活動，更延攬國內外傑出的插畫家，以多樣的畫風詮釋經典文學與現代兒童文學創作。極佳的創意與品質，不僅屢獲國內外大獎，也吸引世界各國翻譯出版他的作品。

　　1996年，郝廣才成為「波隆那國際兒童書插畫展」有史以來最年輕，也是亞洲的第一位評審。

　　《智慧的長河──釋迦牟尼》是他的最新創作。郝廣才表示，他描述的重點在於佛陀為什麼要出家，是因為佛陀有帶領眾生，渡過生死苦難的慈悲心。這種慈悲心，應該對每個人都有所啟示才對。

繪者介紹
保羅艾坦(Paolo D'Altan)

　　保羅艾坦以繪製壯麗景色獨步插畫界，曾獲1992及1993年義大利美術編輯俱樂部金牌及銅牌獎。

　　1964年，保羅艾坦出生於義大利米蘭，自學校畢業後即投入插畫創作事業。由於他很欣賞文藝復興及印象派大師的作品風格，所以他的畫風在現代感的表現方法之外，也有古典藝術的莊嚴質地。

　　《智慧的長河──釋迦牟尼》一書中，他嘗試使用電腦繪圖，用色和構圖雖然比以前更加揮灑自如，細膩的部份依舊令人感動。

BUDDHA

About 2,500 years ago in the north of India a great sage was born. People called him the "Buddha" which meant man of great enlightenment.

The Buddha's father, Cuddhodana was the maharaja of a warrior caste the Sakyas. The Sakyas lived in the principality of Kapilavastu, in a region that is now southern Nepal. The city of Kapilavastu was built high on a mountaintop and from a distance looked as though it was floating amongst the clouds.

Buddha's mother was the maharajahnee. Her name was Mayadevi. It is said that she dreamt one night that a white elephant flew down from the moon-lit sky into her bed and that not long afterwards she discovered herself pregnant.

Ten months later Mayadevi gave birth to a baby under a large tree beside the road on her way to visit her parents. He was given the name Siddhartha, who would later become the Buddha.

Legend has it that after Siddhartha was born, an ascetic monk came to visit Cuddhodana. He saw Siddhartha and praised, "Your Maharaja, your son is going to be a great saint. He will abandon the crown and become a monk, seeking out the truth of life. He's the only one who can eliminate people's vexation and ease their pain. I am too old to listen to his profound preaching. What a pity." Afterwards, Cuddhodana became worried about his son.

Siddhartha grew up a prince, very good at studying and martial art. His father built him three palaces, where flowers blossomed all the time. Those who served Siddhartha were young and beautiful. Cuddhodana wished his son could lived happily in the palaces, so that he would never think of going out and becaming a monk.

Siddhartha never saw the outside world; he travelled from palace to palace in an enclosed carriage. He never thought this strange; believing that everyone lived like him.

When Siddhartha was nineteen his father held a grand banquet in the palace to which he invited all the young women of the city. During the banquet Siddhartha fell in love with the beautiful Yasodhara.

Siddhartha's father approached Yasodhara's father about marriage, but her father insisted that Siddhartha consent to a test before he would allow his daughter to marry.

The first test was in arts and literature. Siddhartha fluently recited sixty-four religious texts, easily outperforming all the other examinees. The second test was in mathematics and Siddhartha answered every question correctly. The third test was of physical strength. Siddhartha threw every opponent to the ground. No one could beat him. The final test was in archery, but Siddhartha broke every bow until his father brought him a large, heavy one from the temple. Siddhartha's arrow flew further than all the rest.

After passing these tests Siddhartha and Yasodhara celebrated their marriage in a ceremony that lasted ten days and nights.

Siddhartha lived a life of total contentment. One day, while in the garden, he noticed the gardener at work, weeding the flowerbeds and transplanting new seedlings. Curious, he asked the gardener what he was up to. The gardener replied,

"The Maharajah likes the plants to be replaced before the flowers die."

"Die? What does that mean?" asked Siddhartha.

The gardener gave a quick laugh, having no way of explaining to the prince the meaning of death. This laugh, like a stone thrown into a pond, unsettled Siddhartha for a moment, but he soon forgot it.

Sometime later, a singer came to perform for Siddhartha. She sang beautifully but there was sadness in her voice. Siddhartha felt there was something strange in her song, but as he had never encountered sadness he did not recognize what it was. He asked her about the song and she replied,

"It is a song about my hometown. I feel homesick every time I sing it."

Siddhartha began to wonder, "What is the rest of the world like? Are there places more lovely than here? Why have I never thought of venturing beyond these walls?"

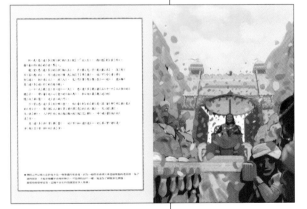

Siddhartha went to his father and told him of his wish to see the world outside. His father had expected this and was well prepared for it. He ordered that all the old, sick and poor be rounded up and removed from the area Siddhartha would pass through.

On the day of his 29th birthday Siddhartha, riding in a carriage carried by thirty-six people and taking with him his beloved white horse and his favorite servant Chandaka, left the city of Kapilavastu for the first time.

Everywhere he went Siddhartha found the houses freshly painted, the people beautifully dressed, healthy and happy. They showered him with rose petals and called his name. He was overjoyed. He had no idea that everything had been carefully stage-managed by his father.

Then just as he was about to return to the palace he caught a glimpse of two unusual creatures down a narrow alley to his left. They were shaped like human beings but were so stooped that their backs seemed broken. Moreover, their hair was thin and sparse, their skin spotted and scarred, their bones protruded cruelly and they had lost most of their teeth.

Siddhartha asked Chandaka, "What are those creatures?"

"People! People like us," replied Chandaka.

"People? Really? Then why do they look like that?" asked Siddhartha.

"They are old, Your Highness."

"What is old?"

"As the years pass by people get older and older. They lose their beauty, strength and memory. It is something that happens to everyone, no one escapes," Chandaka explained. People get old; flowers die. Deeply disturbed, a very silent Siddhartha returned to the palace.

The young prince could not ignore the doubts growing in his mind and so not long after this he left the palace again, riding on his white horse with Chandaka beside him. Soon they came across a woman coughing uncontrollably and spitting blood.

Greatly shocked, Siddhartha asked Chandaka, "What's wrong with her?"

"She's ill and in pain," replied Chandaka.

"Ill," another new word! Next they came upon some men carrying a decaying body and Siddhartha's horse reared in alarm.

"What is that?" he asked Chandaka.

"Your Highness, it's better you don't know," replied Chandaka.

"Tell me!" replied Siddhartha angrily, "I order you!"

Chandaka had no choice. He drew Siddhartha to the side of the road where many bodies wrapped in white cloth were lying on wooden stretchers. A fire had been lit and was beginning to consume the bodies.

"This is death, Your Highness." Chandaka said. "Death is what parts us from our families. It is when we disappear from the world. It brings life to an end."

"Does everyone die?" Siddhartha asked. "Even a maharajah?"

"Yes, everyone, maharajahs, princes, princesses, farmers and beggars, everyone will die."

Music greeted Siddhartha on his return to the palace. His wife had given birth to a son and everyone was celebrating. But Siddhartha had no heart for it. The door to real life had just opened for him and the pain and terror that lay beyond haunted him like a nightmare that would not go away.

Late that night Siddhartha woke to a bright moon. He thought that if he could not find the answer to the mystery of life he would never be happy again. So he decided to leave his loved ones. His children, wife and father. This was the first difficult decision he had ever had to make, but he knew that if he did not leave he would live his whole life a prisoner.

Siddhartha woke the loyal Chandaka, muffled his horses hooves with straw and quietly departed from his home.

Siddhartha and Chandaka left Kapilavastu and began their journey. They traveled for a long time before finally stopping to rest in a grove of trees.

"Chandaka, thank you for accompanying me for such a long time. Now it's time to say goodbye. Go home to my father and my wife and tell them I will not return until I have escaped the suffering of life and death." Siddhartha said.

Crying, Chandaka said, "If you leave, think how sad the maharaja and the princess will be? Who's going to teach your son? How can you be so cold-hearted as to leave them by themselves?"

Siddhartha replied, "That's why I want to find the way to get rid of this pain. Happiness and love seem to be a brief dream. Unavoidably, we'll all separate with people we love one day. I want to save people from pain. If I succeed, I'll return to the palace." Then, Siddhartha immediately drew his gilded sword and cut off his hair.

He saw five naked men sitting on the bank of a stream. They were begging monks. They rejected all worldly comforts and embraced suffering. They would stay in this place until they have found enlightenment. Siddhartha walked into the grove and joined the five monks in their meditations.

For more than six years Siddhartha remained there without uttering a word. He drank rainwater and ate nothing but a little wild food. He was blown by the winds, beaten by the rains, burnt by the sun, and bitten by insects. He grew as thin as a rake but his will remained strong.

One morning he heard the sound of music. He opened his eyes and saw a bamboo raft floating downstream towards him. On it sat an old man playing a flute and a young man playing a seven-stringed lute. The old man suddenly stopped playing and spoke to the younger man.

"Don't tune the strings too tightly or they will break," he said.

These words resounded in Siddhartha's ears like the clang of a bell. He crawled to his feet and step by step slowly entered the river where he began to wash the dirt from his body. A kind young woman passing by offered him a bowl of rice gruel. He ate a few mouthfuls before calling to the five monks.

"Come and eat with me. If you tune it too tightly, the string will break," Siddhartha said.

The five monks, believing he had given in to physical desire, angrily turned their backs and walked away.

Siddhartha smiled for he knew he had made the same mistakes as they did. He sat down under a large tree and began to meditate. He needed to rethink everything, to find a new path to the truth.

How many days did he sit there? How many nights? Siddhartha's mind was visited by images of all kinds: of evil spirits, wild beasts, and beautiful women.

Siddhartha struggled to still his mind until finally the images began to disappear. He opened his eyes and looked at the stars. One by one they too began to disappear. His own "self" also disappeared with them. The sky was emptiness; he was emptiness; everything was emptiness. With this discovery he became the Buddha, the enlightened one.

Having found the truth, Buddha wondered at first whether he should tell others of it. It was not easy to grasp. Could he help others to understand it? He decided he must become a boat that would carry humanity across the great river of suffering.

Thereupon, he went to the five monks and told them of the truth. They became his followers and the Buddha embarked on his 45-year work of bringing enlightenment to the people.

In the Buddha's time Indian society was divided into four castes with the lords and warriors at the top, followed by the priests, then the farmers and business people, and at the bottom the untouchables. Caste was inherited, passed on from one generation to the next. There was no possibility of release.

The caste system was supported by India's religious beliefs. Only the top three castes were allowed to read the scriptures. The untouchables were not permitted to know anything of them and anyone who taught them such things was severely punished no matter what their rank and status.

Buddha wanted to show people another way. He believed that all people were equal and that there should be no social divisions. Moreover, he instructed his followers that they must not merely seek their own salvation. They should also help everyone achieve salvation. He gave spiritual guidance to everyone regardless of their wealth, or status or caste, preaching to all, and accepting tribute from all.

Siddhartha used ingenious methods to explain the truth to people. For example, when a woman came to him weeping and crying because her son had died and she had no wish to go on living, he simply smiled at her and said,

"Go to the village and find a household in which no one has died. Ask them for some mustard seeds, then bring them to me and I will release you from your suffering."

The woman searched the entire village and although everyone was happy to give her the mustard seeds she found no one whom death had not touched. The woman returned to the Buddha and knelt before him saying, "I understand. I won't try to bring my son back to life. Death comes to all of us and I see that now. Teach me, Master. Teach me how to understand the truth of existence."

On another occasion, Buddha came across a man preparing to slaughter a lamb as a sacrifice to the gods. He said to the worshipper, "If you are grateful to the gods for their goodness to you, you ought to offer your own life in sacrifice. What has the lamb got to do with it? Why do you harm it so cruelly?"

The man replied with words from the Hindu scriptures, "Our sacred books say that if a life is sacrificed to the gods its soul will go to heaven. I'm not making it suffer, I am helping it to go to heaven."

Upon hearing this the Buddha replied , "So why not kill your father or your mother or yourself instead? Why miss such a wonderful opportunity to go to heaven, when the lamb may not even want to go?"

The man laid down his knife and said to the Buddha, "You have awakened me. You have made me see the error of my ways."

The Buddha accepted many disciples. He saw them as seeds, seeds of enlightenment and his last words before he died were: "Remember, each and everyone of you is a Buddha." He truly believed that everyone could achieve Buddha-hood and that he had simply set the wheel of the world in motion. The wheel would not stop on his death; there would be others to keep it turning.

The Buddha was followed and respected by thousands of people, but there were others who disliked him. The lords, priests and business people did everything they could to destroy his teachings about equality and preserve the ancient system of castes.

The Buddha's teachings flourished nevertheless. They crossed the mountains to China and thence to Japan, Tibet and Southeast Asia. Today Buddhism is the one of the most widely followed religions in the world and those who have attained enlightenment are carrying on the Buddha's truth down the ages.

●English version by Ann James